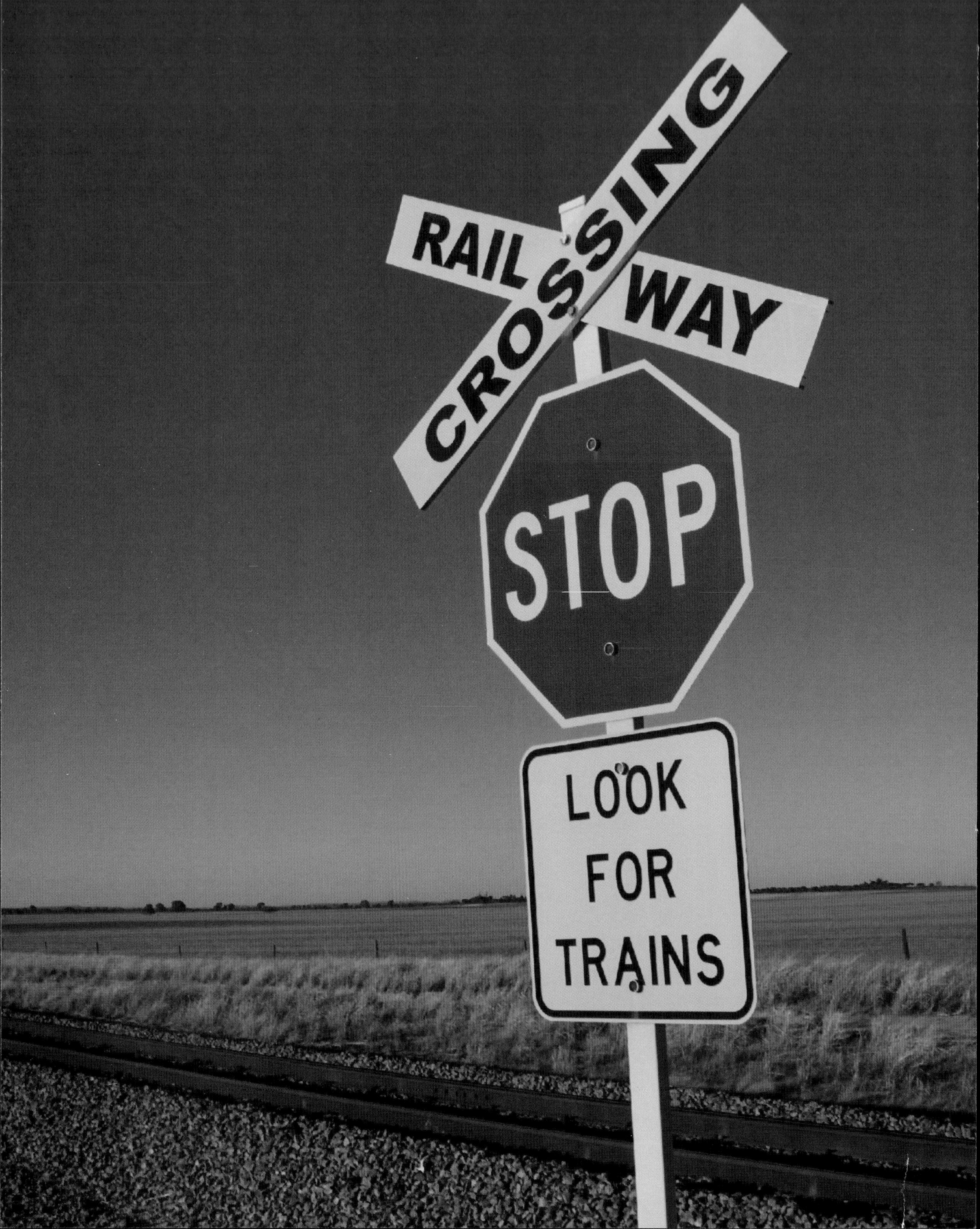
RAILWAY
CROSSING
STOP
LOOK
FOR
TRAINS

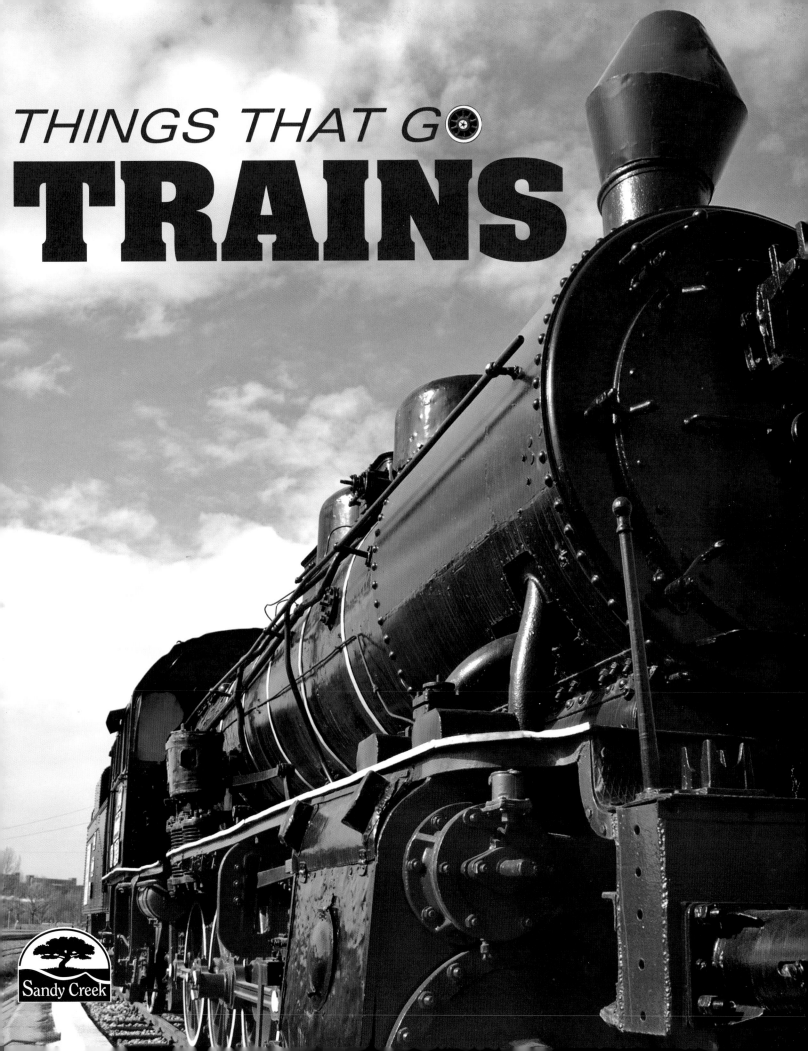

THINGS THAT GO
TRAINS

Written by Catherine Nichols
Designed by Greg Wozney
Photo Researcher Ana Isabel Leal
Packaging Director Susan Knopf
Publishing Director Susan Lurie

Sandy Creek
122 Fifth Avenue
New York, NY 10011

ISBN: 978-1-4351-2736-4

Printed and bound in Singapore
Manufactured March 2011

1 3 5 7 9 10 8 6 4 2

Picture Credits

The publisher would like to thank the following for their kind permission
to reproduce their photographs:

ABBREVIATIONS:
t-top, b-bottom, r-right, l-left, c-center, i-inset, bg-background

Front Cover Algis Balezentis/Shutterstock, Inc.
Endpaper Vlue/Shutterstock, Inc.
Copyright/Table of Contents EcoPrint/Shutterstock, Inc.
Title Page Jarrod Boord/Shutterstock, Inc. (l); Narcis
Parfenti/Shutterstock, Inc. (r)
8-9 James Steidl/Shutterstock, Inc. (8-9bg); Steve Rosset/Shutterstock,
Inc. (9tr); Oleksiy Mark/Shutterstock, Inc. (9cr); Tiggy
Gallery!/Shutterstock, Inc. (9br)
10-11 Dave Wetzel/Shutterstock, Inc. (10bg); Gkuna/Shutterstock, Inc.
(10bi); MPI/Stringer/Archive Photos/Getty Images (10tr); Theunis Jacobus
Botha/Shutterstock, Inc. (11br); Chris Jenner/Shutterstock, Inc. (11bl)
12-13 RonGreer.com/Shutterstock, Inc. (12); Kevin R Williams/Shutterstock,
Inc. (13tr); Igor Grochev/Shutterstock, Inc. (13b)
14-15 Tomasz Darul/Shutterstock, Inc. (14-15bg); Robert
Pernell/Shutterstock, Inc. (14t); 1000 Words/Shutterstock, Inc. (14b);
Robert Kyllo (15tl); Remik44992/Shutterstock, Inc. (15br)
16-17 Lee Prince/Shutterstock, Inc. (16); Condor 36/Shutterstock, Inc.
(17t); Betty Conant/Acclaim Images (17c); FPG/Getty Images (17b)
18-19 Science and Society Picture Library/Getty Images (18); AFP/Getty
Images (19l); Bloomberg/Getty Images (19r)
20-21 Shi Yali/Shutterstock, Inc. (20-21bg); Brian K/Shutterstock, Inc.
(20bi); Christian Lagerek/Shutterstock, Inc. (21li); Nikkitok/Shutterstock,
Inc. (21ri)
22-23 Mamahoohooba/Shutterstock, Inc. (22-23bg); Noboru
Hashimoto/Corbis News/Corbis Sygma (23ti); Holger
Mette/Shutterstock, Inc. (23bi)
24-25 Amy K Planz/Shutterstock, Inc. (24); Anton Foltin/Shutterstock,
Inc. (25t); LazarevaEl/Shutterstock, Inc. (25b)
26-27 Gr8/Shutterstock, Inc. (26-27bg); Ssguy/Shutterstock, Inc. (26li);
Losevsky Pavel/Shutterstock, Inc. (26ri); Jan Kranendonk/Shutterstock,
Inc. (27t); Wolfgang Amri/Shutterstock, Inc. (27bi)
28 Stefan Ataman/Shutterstock, Inc. (28cl); Holger Mette/Shutterstock,
Inc. (28tr); Atref/Shutterstock, Inc. (28b)
Back Cover Vlue/Shutterstock, Inc.

Contents

All Aboard!

Have you ever been on a train? Trains are fun to ride—and fun to read about too! There are many different kinds of trains. They clatter across the countryside, zoom below the city streets in tunnels, or race high above our heads along the rails as they move people and things from place to place.

The first railroads were built in Europe. In the 1500s, wooden rails were placed outside mines so that horse-drawn wagons filled with heavy metals like iron could be pulled easily over the dirt roads. Two hundred years later, steel rails replaced the wooden ones, but horses still provided the pulling power. It wasn't until February 21, 1804, that the first railway journey took place. On this historic day, a **locomotive** pulling five wagons filled with iron chugged along nine miles of rail in Great Britain. From these simple beginnings, trains have developed into the many different kinds you see today.

Steamed Up

The first locomotives were powered by steam. Richard Trevithick, an English engineer, built the first steam locomotive in 1804. Trevithick's amazing invention opened up a whole new way of traveling.

The Power of Steam

A steam locomotive works by harnessing the power of steam. A coal fire is burned in a firebox, which heats water in a boiler. The hot water turns to steam. The steam moves a **piston** back and forth. A driving rod and crank connected to the piston turn the wheels. Coal and water have to be carried on the train to provide this constant source of fuel.

driving rod

piston

crank

Tom Thumb

An American-built steam locomotive was test-driven on the Baltimore and Ohio Railroad in 1830. On a summer's day, the small four-wheel locomotive, called Tom Thumb, chugged along the tracks at 18 miles per hour pulling a car filled with passengers. On the return trip, the driver of a horse-driven car challenged Tom Thumb to an unofficial race—and the car won! No matter, in a few years time, steam locomotives were the main form of long-distance transportation in the United States.

This fireman is shoveling more coal into the firebox.

The Fireman

While the engineer drove the train, it was the fireman's job to make sure there was enough steam to keep the train moving. He did this by stoking and feeding the fire and by checking that there was always water in the boiler.

Pressure gauges help a fireman check to see that enough steam is being made.

FAST FACTS

The fastest steam locomotive was the *Mallard*. It reached 125 mph on July 3, 1938, as it sped between the cities of Grantham and Peterborough in England.

Moving Forward

Steam locomotives were dirty, noisy, and expensive to operate so people began to look for better ways to travel by rail. One way was with trains pulled by a diesel-electric locomotive. Another way was with trains run totally by electricity. Both are still in use today.

Diesel-fueled Trains

In the 1930s, steam locomotives began to be replaced with ones that ran on **diesel fuel**. Diesel-electric locomotives have many advantages over steam. They cost less to run and to maintain, and they can go faster than steam locomotives. Plus, they are quieter, and they don't produce the dirt and heat that steam locomotives did.

FAST FACTS

A diesel-electric engine is about 50 times more powerful than the engine of a car.

How a Diesel Engine Works

A steam engine directly turns a locomotive's wheels. A diesel-electric engine works differently. A diesel-fueled generator makes electricity, which powers an electric motor that is used to turn the wheels. These engines are enormous and can weigh more than 20 tons.

Powered by Electricity

While a diesel-electric train must generate its own electricity onboard, an electric train uses electricity from an outside source. Some electric trains pick up electrical power from overhead cables. Other electric trains get electricity from an extra rail in the track called a **third rail**.

The *pantograph* on top of this electric train collects the high-voltage current from the overhead cables to power the train.

Staying on Track

Trains need tracks to run. Millions of miles of tracks crisscross the continents. The trains that travel on them take passengers safely to their destinations and move tons of freight from place to place all over the world.

Tracks are laid on top of a layer of crushed stone called *ballast*.

Making Tracks

Most tracks have two steel rails that support and guide the train. The rails rest on top of concrete or wood slats called **ties**. Spikes attach the rails to the ties and hold them in place.

Steel Wheels

A train wheel is made from steel and has two rims of unequal size. The larger rim is called a **flange**. It holds the wheel firmly on the rail and stops it from slipping off the tracks.

Clickety-clack Tracks

Until recently, most tracks had jointed rails. Jointed rails were long pieces of rails bolted together with steel plates. Small gaps were left between the rail ends so that in hot weather the steel ends had room to expand. If you see a train today riding on these tracks, you'll hear a clickety-clack sound as they pass over each gap. Nowadays high-speed trains run on tracks made from steel that's been welded to make one continuous rail. Since very few joints are used, trains running on these tracks give smoother, quieter rides.

Derailed!

Sometimes a train derails. That means it comes off its rails. This kind of accident can cause a lot of damage and can injure passengers. Why do trains derail? The rails might be broken or are not aligned properly, or sometimes the train is going too fast and it jumps the rails. Trains can also derail if they collide with an obstacle on the tracks or with another train.

Going the Distance

Some passenger trains travel long distances. These kinds of trips can take many, many days so travelers need places to sleep, eat, and relax. Special cars on these trains help make long-distance travel comfortable.

FAST FACTS

The world's longest train trip is 5,778 miles long. It's the Trans-Siberian Express, and it stops at 91 stations in nine days. The train starts in Moscow and runs through the Russian countryside, ending in Vladivostok on the east coast.

Meals on Wheels

Most long-distance trains have a dining car where passengers can go for breakfast, lunch, and dinner. Sometimes the meals are prepared beforehand and just reheated and served aboard the train. For in-between times, snacks and drinks are available in the lounge car.

Observation car

At the rear of many long-distance trains are observation cars. Large windows let passengers take in the scenic views.

Sleeping Cars

George Pullman invented the Pullman sleeping car. It came out in 1865. With places to sleep on a train, long-distance train travel was now easier. Weary travelers could get a good night's sleep, and the beds, called berths, didn't take up extra space. Pullman **porters** were on hand to help passengers both night and day.

The Lap of Luxury

Some long-distance railroad companies go out of their way to pamper their passengers. Of course, not every passenger can afford this kind of first-class luxury, but if you can't take a luxury train ride, it's cool to read about them too!

This carriage was fit for a queen. Really! It was built in 1869 for Britain's Queen Victoria by the London and North Western Railway.

FAST FACTS

The *Orient Express* crossed six continents in its original route, spanning more than 1,500 miles.

Food and drink for the passengers of the *Orient Express* took up so much space they were carried in a separate railroad car.

20th Century Limited

Considered by many train experts to be the greatest passenger train, the *20th Century Limited* ran from New York City to Chicago starting in 1902. A red carpet was rolled out for passengers getting on and off the train. Men boarding the train were presented with carnations and women were given perfume and flowers. Haircuts were available on the train, and business people could dictate letters to secretaries, whose services were provided by the railroad. In 1967, the *20th Century Limited* pulled out of New York's Grand Central Station for the last time.

The Blue Train

South Africa's *Blue Train* started its 1,000 mile-journey from Pretoria to Cape Town in 1936 and it is still running today. Known as a moving 5-star hotel, passengers can enjoy 24-hour butler service, relax in soundproof suites, and watch the train's journey through a camera positioned at the front of the train.

Orient Express

The famous *Orient Express* provided the height of luxury when it first started in 1883. Running from Paris to Istanbul, the train had three wood-paneled coaches, marble sinks with gold plumbing, and a library. Crystal chandeliers hung in the dining car and tables were set with the finest china and silver. As they ate, diners were entertained with live music. In 1977, the train made its last Paris to Istanbul run. Over the next thirty years, the length of the route was shortened bit by bit. Eventually the train only traveled between Strasbourg, Germany, and Vienna, Austria. On December 12, 2009, the *Orient Express* took off from Strasbourg for the last time and the great train stopped running altogether.

Faster Than a Speeding Bullet

Whoosh! While most typical passenger trains travel at under 100 mph, high-speed trains average around 150 mph. And some new models can go much, much faster.

Built for Speed

A high-speed train is built to go fast. That's why its front is shaped like a jet plane. This streamlined design makes it easy for the train to move through air.

Cabins on high-speed trains are airtight and soundproof.

Futuristic Works of Art

High-speed trains come in many streamlined shapes. Their futuristic design is something the designers of the original steam trains never could have imagined. The materials used to manufacture these trains are also much different than those that were used years ago. Lightweight materials such as fiberglass and carbon fiber have replaced iron and steel.

High-Wire Act

Some high-speed trains are powered from wires high above the train.

FAST FACTS

Some high-speed trains are designed to tilt from side to side as they round curves.

The first high-speed train ran in Japan. The *Shinkansen*, also known as the bullet train, opened its doors to passengers in 1964.

The Future of Train Travel

A new type of technology is changing the way we travel by train. A few countries are using powerful magnets to run high-speed trains that can go as fast as 300 mph—and sometimes faster.

Opposites Attract

The maglev is a high-speed train that doesn't need wheels. It's called "maglev" because magnets are used to levitate, or raise, the train above the track, or **guideway**. Magnets placed in the train and in the track push against each other. This creates a force that raises the train above its track and pushes it forward. Because there is no friction between the train and the tracks, the train can travel at speeds of more than 300 mph.

Maglev trains provide passengers with a smooth, quiet ride.

FAST FACTS

Most maglev trains rise an inch or two off the ground. Japanese maglev trains rise almost 4 inches. However, these trains must use rubber wheels until they reach liftoff speed.

Some maglevs don't need drivers. Instead, a computer controls the trains.

Super Magnets, Super Train

Japan's MLX01 maglev train uses superconducting magnets. These magnets allowed it to reach a speed of 361 mph in a test run— a world record! For the train to work properly, the magnets must be kept at below-freezing temperatures. The super powerful magnets can conduct electricity even after power has been shut off, saving energy costs.

The Train to the Plane

China's Transrapid was the first maglev to provide service for passengers. It started in 2003, and it takes passengers from the city of Shanghai to Shanghai's airport.

Getting to Work

How do people get to work or to school? For many, the answer is by train. Commuter trains are a fast and efficient way to travel to and from a city center. Often, commuter trains share tracks with freight trains and long-distance passenger trains.

Up in the Air

Monorails are trains that travel on a single rail or beam. The train straddles the rail, which rests on towers many feet above the ground. The rail provides the electric power that runs the train. Many riders use monorails to commute to work or school.

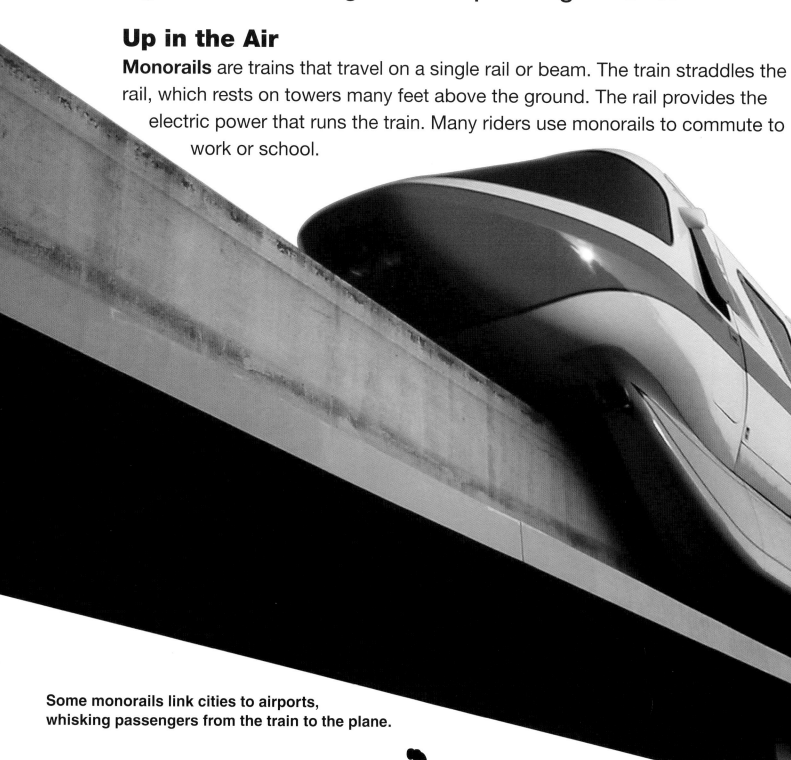

Some monorails link cities to airports, whisking passengers from the train to the plane.

Light Rail

Light rails are trains that run on tracks along city streets and can be powered either by overhead cables or by an electric rail. Some light rail trains share the road with cars and other vehicles. Riders use them to get to work and to travel around the city.

Traveling by light rail reduces car traffic. Because the trains are powered by electricity, they help the environment, too.

Which End Is Which?

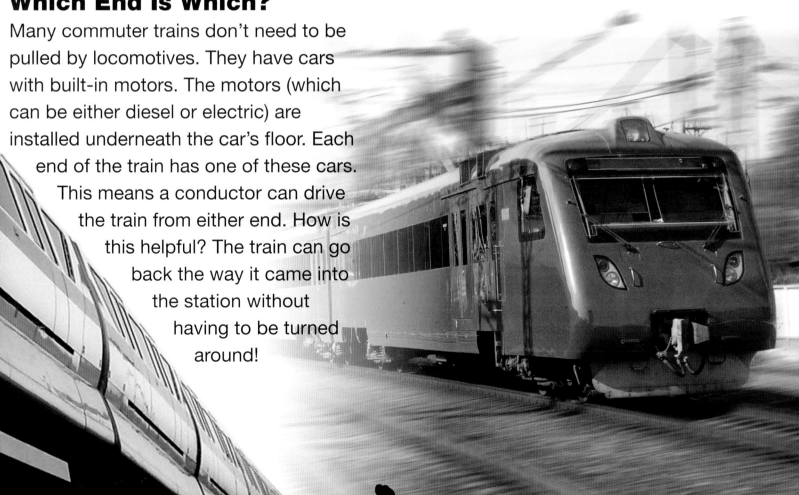

Many commuter trains don't need to be pulled by locomotives. They have cars with built-in motors. The motors (which can be either diesel or electric) are installed underneath the car's floor. Each end of the train has one of these cars. This means a conductor can drive the train from either end. How is this helpful? The train can go back the way it came into the station without having to be turned around!

Rapid Transit

In cities, trains have to travel in underground tunnels or on elevated tracks above the city streets. These train systems can move lots of people around the city, day and night. They are called rapid transit systems.

Down Below

Underground rapid transit systems are common in big cities. Riders use stairs, elevators, or escalators to reach underground train stations where they can board the trains. But first they must buy tickets or tokens to pay for their trip!

Rush Hour

During morning and evening hours subways are crowded with people rushing to and from work. In some of Japan's most crowded subway lines, platform attendants wearing white gloves push riders into the trains' cars so that the doors can close.

Up Above

Some cities have trains that run on elevated lines built above the streets. Like underground trains, elevated trains run without the worry of street traffic.

Subway Lines

Underground train systems usually have several lines of trains running along different routes. Some lines connect with each other at certain stations so that riders can transfer from one line to another.

Each line has its own name or number. This NYC subway train runs on the A line and is called the A train.

FAST FACTS

The first subway was the London Underground. On opening day in 1863, about 40,000 people rode the subway.

New York City has the largest subway system in the United States. It has 722 miles of track and 468 stations. About 1.3 billion people ride the subway each year.

Record Breakers

There are many amazing trains in the world. But only a few can claim to be the best in their class. Let's take a look at some of these extreme trains.

Highest

At its highest point, the Qinghai-Tibet Railway reaches 16,640 feet. The air is so thin at this altitude, breathing can be difficult and sometimes impossible. To make sure that passengers can breathe, railway engineers designed sealed cabins with regulated oxygen levels. Cabins also come with a separate oxygen supply for each passenger.

Fastest

Running on magnetic-levitation tracks, Japan's JR-Maglev is the world's fastest train. Its top speed has been clocked at 361 mph. France's TGV high-speed train holds the record for fastest wheel-driven train, reaching 357 mph.

Steepest

The steepest railroad is in Switzerland. A mountain train's toothed wheel, or cog, grips the track, allowing it to climb to the top of Mount Pilatus at an altitude of 6,995 feet. At its steepest, the track rises to 48 degrees. That's as steep as a playground slide!

Glossary

ballast crushed rock that is used to make a bed for railroad tracks

diesel fuel a fuel used to power diesel engines

flange a metal lip on a train's wheel that helps keep the train on the rails

guideway a track that a maglev train is propelled along

light rail a train that runs on tracks through city streets

locomotive a wheeled machine that moves under its own power to pull train cars

maglev a high-speed train that uses magnetic levitation as its power to move forward

monorail a train that runs on a single rail

pantograph a device that collects electric current from overhead power lines for electric trains to use

piston a rod that fits into a larger rod and is moved back and forth under the force of some sort of pressure, such as steam

porter an attendant on a sleeping car who waits on passengers and maintains the berths

tie a rectangular slat made from wood or concrete that is used as a base for railroad tracks

third rail a rail built alongside train tracks that provides power to an engine

Index